21st Century Vision of Management Leadership

Ethics and Values

Ramaswamy Thanu

Printed by CreateSpace
An Amazon Company

Introduction

This book briefly seeks to identify the basic need of the management profession to ensure effectiveness and results in the age of E Governance for resource utilization. It lays stress on imparting ethics and value systems in management enlarging the scope of the profession in framing solutions for chronic problems of society richly drawing from the treasure of ancient wisdom.

Contents

1. Corruption and poverty alleviation

E Governance has many laudable objectives and beneficial results. Procedures have been simplified considerably. The common man has experienced most of the benefits as in the case of railway reservations.

Forms of corruption include bribery, extortion, nepotism, patronage, graft, and embezzlement. This creates great social injustice particularly to the poor sections of the population. Corruption poses a serious development challenge. It undermines good governance by subverting formal processes. Corruption in the judiciary compromises the rule of law and that in public administration results in the unfair provision of services. It corrodes and erodes the institutional capacity of government. Corrupt practices influence decision-making particularly involving huge financial outlays. It undermines economic development by causing all round distortions and inefficiency. In the private sector, corruption jacks up the cost of business through the price of illegal payments, the management fee of negotiating with officials. Though some people observe that corruption reduces costs by eliminating red tape, the availability of bribes induces officials to devise ingeniously new rules and engineer delays.

While corruption inflates the cost of business, it also distorts the playing field, shielding firms with connections from competition and thereby sustaining inefficient firms. Cases are not rare where firms supplying first quality products and services are disqualified in favor of those who are substandard because they could pay off huge amounts as bribes.

Corruption also lowers compliance with construction, environmental, or other regulations, reduces the quality of government services and infrastructure, and increases budgetary pressures on government. Siphoning of resources and the resultant wastage thwart the main objectives of good governance.

World economic progress, in general, during the last decade has been remarkable. Productivity and employment have increased in many fields and industrial growth has been over 9% in some countries. Globalization has brought easy and abundant availability of goods and services in the country. Some countries have foreign exchange reserves of over $250 billion. The stock markets are booming with activity and massive inflow of investment from abroad takes place. But corruption also gets a boost eating away part of the resources earmarked for development.

2. Managerial leadership

The effectiveness of managerial leadership is affected by the predominance of corruption in all areas of activity setting aside, professional integrity and ethics. This prevents level playing field for those who believe in fair business practices. Thus the best of expertise becomes non-usable. Wastage of resource arises on account of governmental activity driven by corruption and greed. This creates a chain reaction bringing the evil effects of corruption all through the hierarchy down to the lowest level. Apart from causing depletion of resources, this promotes wide disparity in incomes and growth. Corruption and greed of the officialdom choke decision-making and create obstacles in the way of economic progress though it is said to act as an expediting process.

The democratic system as it functions today in some countries does not permit penetration of professionalism in politics with the most appropriate skills. It is devoid of ethics. Countries like Singapore where the politicians occupying ministerial posts are high caliber professionals are few. The exclusion of politicians from the network of developing core competence for ruling the country and managing the economy distorts the system. Exceptions are rare.

This takes us to the question of widening the scope of managerial leadership and area of responsibilities. Corporate leadership is concerned with conservation and optimum utilization of resources. Does the management profession have any responsibility for devising ways and means of improving performance in developing core competence and national progress? The seeds of corruption are sown in the minds of men. They are nurtured by the flush of funds originating through corrupt means of party funding which is not subject to audit and scrutiny. This encourages a chain of hierarchies, creating powerful and unbreakable links with officials and donors who disrupt the sound management of the economy. The gravitational pull of such negative leadership downwards slows down progress and performance.

Inadequacies in professional skills at the top layers of the government and the dominance of vested interests, act as an insulated shield preventing the penetration of most effective managerial tools.

Luckily the IT industry is comparatively free from the menace of political interference. Politicians do not tamper with it because many are not familiar with the complexity of the industry. Further Companies, which have achieved tremendous growth and success, attribute their achievement due to their philosophy of being value driven and not greed driven. The management of such companies has been able to resist pressures from the government officials to dilute the standard of ethics in dealings.

Can corporate leadership effectively help to tackle the twin evil of corruption and poverty? Is there any set of effective tools they can design and adopt? If so how can it be done and how soon. Can this be made as part of the vision for the 21st century for all countries? These questions take us to the objective of *widening the scope of conceptual skill* which is the ability to think creatively about, analyze and understand complicated and abstract ideas. Using a well developed conceptual skill set, top level business managers need to be able to look at their company as a holistic entity, to see the interrelationships between its divisions, and to understand how the firm fits into and affects its overall environment .Enlarging the skill should include ideas to demolish the pillars of Corruption and promote E Governance which has brought benefits to the common man with prospects of greater benefits and convenience.

3. The Need

Corporate leadership

Corporate leadership has to accept a major role in national planning and reconstruction. Planning is concerned with utilizing resources most productively. India's ancient heritage upholds the cause of humanity. The concepts and principles of administration and human conduct framed thousands of years ago had that end in view. They hold good even now.

Corporate leadership and conceptual skill need a wider definition to include imbibing the value system imbedded in our heritage and scriptures. We have to dig out and apply those with modification, convert them into productive tools to suit present day conditions. These are in the areas of time management, motivation, communications, organizational behavior, avoidance of conflict, human welfare, sustainable living standards, life balance, conservation of resources and environment.

Leaders will do well to widen the horizon of thinking and evolve tools and techniques to tackle the problem of corruption and poverty alleviation. While it is laudable to have billionaires among the middle class, it is also necessary in the interests of stability and harmony in society; those below the poverty level are lifted up economically. Those who manage the national economy need more of professional content in their decision making. The political content has to be minimized. It is this political content, of high dosage, which brings in its train all vices. It introduces unfair and unethical practices feeding the machine of corruption causing it to spread its tentacles far and wide.

This calls for new leadership objectives. These have to go beyond corporations and organizations and include political organizations particularly in the area of development leadership. The built in hurdles for social harmony and progress have to be identified, pointed out, studied and remedial measures recommended. Professionally independent body can do this in the national interest.

Management leadership should look beyond business and industry. Ethics and character come from spiritual outlook and they play a vital role in harmonious, sure and sustained economic development. This constitutes the core resource development strategy. It is developing the individual in whatever capacity he is, using the value based concepts, techniques and tools drawn from our ancient wisdom realizing the potential of the mind, body and intellect. It will help to achieve better life balance and harmony.

Poverty elimination is an important area where they have to evolve new tools. Education is another area. Similarly with social harmony they have to play a role. They have to devise tools for improvements in law and order and for effective functioning of the judiciary within the constitutional provisions. Dogmas and conventional tools are becoming obsolete. We should not give a stone when one wants bread.

4. Systems approach

Management welcomes knowledge from all disciplines. It believes in an inter-disciplinary approach. It upholds the systems approach for solving problems. It has widely applied the systems approach for solving problems in industry. In the area of corruption and poverty elimination too there are vital subsystems. They remain outside the system and disrupt the fulfillment of the objective of economic growth with equity and social harmony. These include the politicians, the legislature and the judiciary.

A systems approach incorporating the value system for demolishing corruption in organizations- political, social and economic will be productive of results. This will ensure right leadership, for thrust will be given using training methods to promote development leadership. The profession of management has to go beyond corporate governance and corporate leadership. It should focus on developing leaders for political excellence which will ultimately benefit business substantially.

5. Spiritual Strength

One important area of knowledge demanding close and immediate attention is application of ethics in management. Such ethics derive strength from spirituality. In fact contrary to popular belief this is totally secular and universally beneficial. This has recently gained acceptance in western countries as a tool of managerial effectiveness. Countries and organizations where officials take orders from a situation and not from individuals have benefited from using such tools.

While developing all these aspects the unseen resource of spiritual strength - that is belief in the spirit behind the three faculties, which makes them function, is to be respected and relied upon. We may call it life, energy or consciousness. Any work in any field of activity if done with this vision will bring better results. It will make any professional a better professional in his field. It will be done with a sense of dedication. Great men and leaders who made tremendous contribution to the country were those who had strengths deeply rooted in spirituality. They were motivated to excel in their performance through a sense of fulfillment and they acted far beyond enriching themselves.

Enlarged conceptual skill was imbedded in them and they could visualize the country as one integrated whole. They practiced sustainability by respecting environmental forces.

Twenty first century is going to be the century *fusing economic progress with spiritual strength*. It augurs well for the world economy. Countries with spiritual strength hold the beacon of hope and leadership for world development. Wisdom and the heritage of the past dating back to thousands of years teach us the art of human development and excellence. This is the unique strength India has, which others are yet to acquire. If man is developed to attain excellence, the family, society, nation, country and the whole world will attain better growth and harmony. This lies at the core of the conceptual skill. Concepts like Dharma Management have surfaced and found greater acceptance. Real values of life do contain potential for improving the quality of human resource, which commands other resources. India's rich heritage and wisdom provide ample evidence of this potential. There is no need to feel shy about using such beneficial tools and management can freely make use of them.

6. Human development

So the most important aspect of human development is to develop man to attain his maximum potential. His assets are the body, mind and intellect the three pillars on which his excellence is built. Intellect can be trained to develop positive thinking ensuring right decisions. The mind can be developed to imbibe values, which will benefit humanity. The body can be kept healthy so that work can be done at peak efficiency with little down time.

.

Optimum utilization of resources implies prevention of wastage. Breakdown of law and order is a major source of such loss. How can management produce maximum results in terms of national benefits? What is the most valuable tool for the manager? Are we sincerely and steadily striving for human excellence in all areas of activity? The existing tools, techniques and concepts are inadequate. This is seen from the prevalence of corruption and corporate frauds, which globally exist.

7. The Tool

Human body as a chariot

Some universities in Western countries are giving importance to introducing values and spiritual orientation to management practices. Corporate leadership will benefit if they realize the relevance and strength of the core values that substantially help to attain human excellence. Here skill to consider the human body as a chariot with several interrelationships becomes very important.

.The ancient wisdom contained in our scriptures focuses on developing the inner strengths of the body, mind and intellect. The analogy of the human body to the chariot gives an invaluable insight.

The wheels of the chariot represent Dharma (righteousness) which is the foundation for other goals, namely, Artha and Kama. The horses represent the senses, the reins the mind, the charioteer the intellect and the flag with the image of Hanuman symbolizing a force overcoming obstacles with the determination to achieve the goals. The senses are controlled by the mind and the mind in turn is controlled by the intellect.

The planning and directing function manifest in basing all actions on Dharma (righteousness). Artha or earning of wealth and Kama or fulfilling desires are subject to Dharma. This principle, if understood and faithfully followed will eliminate greed or curtail it significantly. Wealth created will be used for the benefit of a larger section of people within and outside the organization. Corporate social responsibility will be automatically ensured. It will be wealth creation with sustainability and according to priority.

The discriminating intellect sifts relevant knowledge, assigns priority, and arrives at right conclusions and sound decisions. The control function is exercised by pulling back the senses (horses) to the right track with the reins (mind) i.e. correcting deviations from the main objective.

8. Benefits

If the analogy of the chariot and its relation to the human body is understood and assimilated by all the employees in the organization compliance of decisions will be easy and effective. With more and more employees at all levels in the organization practicing such principles the results will be better and far reaching. This perspective gives a new dimension to management and managerial skills. This is enlarging the dimensions of the conceptual skill.

Ancient times witnessed rulers and leaders who were men of integrity, vision and concern for the people's prosperity with harmony. They had the noblest and widest concept of conceptual skill which was reflected in the maxim *Loka samastha sukhino bhavantu*. They set examples of honest living and strong concern for the people. Unfortunately very little is done now for promoting the role of character in economic development and in nation building.

The only remedy for arresting corruption is to impart a value system along with other tools and techniques of management. If corporate leadership can identify the causes for poor performance with a view to improve and bring out the results in public they can have an impact on the quality of governance marking a beginning of the process of demolition of the fortress of corruption .

A well designed management control system can bring substantial improvement to minimize the impact of corruption. This facilitates early detection of fraudulent practices. This is all the more easy when real time computerized control systems are possible. Human excellence should be the goal of all organizations. Only if the top political layers in government and administration have the will to implement measures to achieve excellence, beneficial results will percolate and prevail in all organizations and hierarchies.

9. Value system

The value system definitely provides answers to many problems of administration and human relationships. They seek to ensure good conduct, fairness and equity in administration and healthy human relationships. Here quantitative and other techniques fail. We have to develop an open mind to be convinced about their worth, relevance and applicability. *We must embrace the maxim "Let noble thoughts come to us from all sides".*

We don't have to search for new tools. Actually we have only to discover the essential and most productive tools from India's ancient heritage without being prejudiced. Indian value system is the greatest global asset. It is the springboard for character formation and ultimately human destiny. This is clear from the following verse.

Sow a thought and reap an idea,
Sow an idea and reap an act,
Sow an act and reap a character
Sow a character and reap a destiny.

10. Self-management

It is essential for the healthy and sustained growth of the economy and for improving the standard of living of the poorer sections of the population that the tool of *self-management* techniques is given wide application by leaders. India's rich heritage with an ocean of sacred literature contains enough material for unearthing tools and concepts of relevance to modern conditions and times.

The exclusion of this factor as a subsystem for problem solving has been the cause of retrogression and growth of corruption. This lapse has resulted in system failure and retarded national progress, making it lopsided. Often, there is no national perspective and this lack of conceptual skill on the part of those running the government has resulted in more efforts and time being devoted for resolving conflicts and clash of interests.

Society needs to benefit by cost effective recommendations and results flowing from implementation. Policy makers have to make changes in polices to permit management to choose any area for study where social benefits will be considerable and in the national interest.

Academics and professionals can evolve new areas of research, which include a reliable systems approach to solution of national problems bringing in its fold the world of waste generation and willful resource annihilation.

The conventional tools apart, tools from ancient wisdom of this land can be taken and developed. This will strengthen the declaration of management that it welcomes knowledge from all disciplines and the discipline of ethics and spirituality will be brought within its fold. This will definitely be a value addition to professional knowledge.

E governance could be supplemented and facilitated by management concepts and tools with high ethical and spiritual content to attain human excellence and resource utilization. Such concepts are readily available in our scriptures like Bhagavad-Gita On-line real time information will help to expedite the decision making process and reduce the opportunity for champions of corruption to exploit the delays converting them into money and benefits. Other measures desirable are:

Persuading national leaders to adopt management tools, which will increase the professional content in their decisions and ensure social harmony and progress?

Bring out research findings of studies on benefits and havoc caused by good/poor leadership and recommend remedial measures.

Including corporate leaders forming units for specialized study and research on social harmony, law and order, development leadership

Forming a National Social Security Fund to benefit the poor

Impart spiritual strength to management to facilitate character formation and promote human excellence.

Politicians should be equipped with the concepts, knowledge, and tools including values to discharge their responsibilities to the people. Value and ethics do have a vital role in attaining human excellence, motivating the followers and conserving resources. Democracy does not advocate wanton wastage of resources by inaction and core incompetence. It does not envisage a form of government by human drainpipes. It is time to draft mature competent selective politicians as part of the management profession to interact and to make them realize what professionals can do for the country.

11.21st Century Conceptual Skill

21st century is destined to be the century of spirituality, which can impart great strength and purpose to human endeavor. In this area India has a great role to play and contribute to world prosperity. It has demonstrated this with the effulgence of its native intelligence and brainpower. It suits the genius of India. Its heritage depicts the finest of values systems, principles of social harmony and motivation to view performance as a source of self-fulfillment.

The heritage if rightly understood and assimilated, offers solutions to all problems of mankind. It is a question of bringing a vast number of people within its disciplined approach. The tools of mind control and positive thinking ensure productivity and equity. It helps to conserve the environment. Leadership quality will considerably improve to turn many politicians into statesmen.

Mankind owes so much to India's ancient wisdom. Works of wisdom like the Bhagavad-Gita contain teachings many of which have management implications particularly in the area of human excellence. There is nothing higher than the Gita as a source of motivation and excellence for nation building and leadership development. Only men of character and vision deeply rooted in sound management principles and ancient wisdom can make a nation culturally and economically strong. This is the objective of self-management.

Any activity turns more productive if spiritual strength is imparted. Management and spirituality are creative pursuits and both stress on optimum resource utilization. While the former deals with external resources the latter develops internal faculties of man.

Our environmentalists discovered the need for conservation of natural wealth only recently whereas India's ancient sages discovered and propagated this concept thousands of years ago. The mind is said to be a $10 billion gift. We must stretch our minds to the farthest limit. This is an extension of the management concept of thinking big.

Conserving our energy and cultivating positive values will greatly help the cause of management. It is the purifier, which will help to liquidate all evil tendencies in the mind. There will be no source of disturbance and one can attain great freedom from stress, which is a malady of the modern executive.

Spiritual strength is the greatest asset of any individual and nation. A manager benefits considerably and attains Total Quality Management by developing and holding on to it. Thus we achieve a better quality of life.

Management profession will grow by leaps and bounds and gain a lot if it brings spirituality in its fold as part of a systems approach to efficient value based and result oriented management. It is worthwhile to remember the formula practiced by the Japanese management i.e., Faith + Discipline + Hard work = Success. This if faithfully followed and with ethics and spiritual strength success will be guaranteed.

When conventional concepts, tools and techniques fail or are found too inadequate, the value system rightly tapped and utilized, will bring success.

An example of positive thoughts is seen in the views expressed by the famous economist and Nobel Laureate, Jan Tinbergen.

". The leading philosophy of the present, which always asks for more material goods and does not attach much value at simplicity of life or modesty in claims, has to be replaced by alternative philosophies and surely much could be learned from Mahatma Gandhi's words and example. The real values of life do contain a sufficient quantity of food and shelter; but it is not necessary to have the luxuries now aimed at. Cultural values will have to be "upgraded" again. How can we have global harmony until then?

While rich nations are achieving higher levels of living in terms of comforts, convenience and material possessions, poor nations are unable to maintain even the existing levels. In this context the views expressed by Jan Tinbergen are of great significance.

Let us hope such an approach and a success formula will go global and will be accepted in the near future. May there be peace, prosperity and happiness to all human beings on this planet. This is the theme of enlarged conceptual skill for global harmony.